ALTERNATOR
BOOKS™

THE *FUTURE* IS *FEMALE*

Changemakers in

GOVERNMENT

Women Leading the Way

DR. ARTIKA R. TYNER

T0018882

Lerner Publications ◆ Minneapolis

This book is dedicated to Ellen Johnson Sirleaf for her leadership and service.

Lerner Publications Company
An imprint of Lerner Publishing Group, Inc.
241 First Avenue North
Minneapolis, MN 55401 USA

For reading levels and more information, look up this title at www.lernerbooks.com.

Main body text set in Aptifer Sans LT Pro Medium.
Typeface provided by Linotype AG.

Designer: Athena Currier **Photo Editor:** Nicole Berglund
Lerner team: Martha Kranes

Library of Congress Cataloging-in-Publication Data

Names: Tyner, Artika R., author.
Title: Changemakers in government : women leading the way / Dr. Artika R. Tyner.
Description: Minneapolis, : Lerner Publications, [2024] | Series: The future is female |
   Includes bibliographical references and index. | Audience: Ages 8–12 | Audience:
   Grades 4–6 | Summary: "Discover the women who shaped every branch of the
   United States government as well as those who are leading it today. Readers also
   learn about women leading nations around the globe"— Provided by publisher.
Identifiers: LCCN 2023011252 (print) | LCCN 2023011253 (ebook) |
   ISBN 9798765608876 (library binding) | ISBN 9798765625019 (paperback) |
   ISBN 9798765618301 (epub)
Subjects: LCSH: Women—Political activity—United States—Juvenile literature. |
   Women legislators—United States—Juvenile literature. | Women judges—United
   States—Juvenile literature. | United States—Politics and government—Juvenile
   literature. | BISAC: JUVENILE NONFICTION / Biography & Autobiography / Women
Classification: LCC HQ1236.5.U6 T96 2024 (print) | LCC HQ1236.5.U6 (ebook) |
   DDC 320.082/0973—dc23/eng/20230411

LC record available at https://lccn.loc.gov/2023011252
LC ebook record available at https://lccn.loc.gov/2023011253

Manufactured in the United States of America
1-1009482-51565-4/28/2023

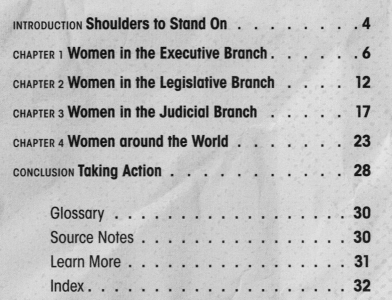

Table of Contents

Shoulders to Stand on

In 1972 Shirley Chisholm stood before a large crowd and declared that she was the "candidate of the people of America." The crowd cheered as she shared her vision for the future. She wanted everyone to have their basic needs met. The hungry would be fed, and the unsheltered would have a place to stay. Children would have quality education, and the sick would receive health care. Chisholm's vision brought people together.

Shirley Chisholm announces her presidential campaign in 1972.

As the first Black woman elected to Congress, in 1968, Chisholm had already broken barriers. She broke even more barriers in 1972 by becoming the first Black woman to run for the presidential nomination on a major party ticket.

Though Chisholm lost her presidential run, she inspired more women to get involved in politics. Vice President Kamala Harris said that she stands on Chisholm's shoulders. This book highlights women leaders in politics. There is not enough room to highlight every important government official in these pages. But the women in this book have fought for what they believe in and provide shoulders for the next generation of leaders to stand on.

CHAPTER 1

Women in the Executive Branch

Women shape every branch of the US government. One of those branches is the executive branch. The executive branch enforces laws. It is made up of the president, vice president, executive office of the president, and the cabinet. Trailblazing women have broken barriers by serving in these roles and speaking up.

Making a Difference

Kamala Harris's mother taught her the importance of helping people in need. Harris carried this with her in her career in

Kamala Harris speaks at an election event in 2020.

public service. In the Senate, she focused on fighting hunger, improving access to quality health care, and supporting immigrants' rights. In 2020 Kamala Harris made history as the

"My mother would look at me and she'd say, 'Kamala, you may be the first to do many things, but make sure you are not the last.'"

—KAMALA HARRIS

first woman, South Asian person, and Black person to become vice president. She is working to create more opportunities for women inside and outside of government.

STANDING UNITED

From 2017 to 2018, Nikki Haley was the US ambassador to the United Nations. In 2023 she announced she was running for president.

Nikki Haley campaigns for president in 2023.

Elaine Chao served in two different presidents' cabinets.

Supporting Workers

In 2001 Elaine Chao became the first Asian American in a president's cabinet. In her eight years as secretary of labor, she protected worker's rights. She promoted safety for workers and protected their retirement money. In 2017 Chao became the secretary of transportation. She worked to improve rural transportation and fix aging rails. She was the secretary of transportation for four years.

LEADING FOREIGN AFFAIRS

In 2005 Condoleezza Rice became the first Black woman secretary of state. She advised the president on international policies from trade to immigration.

Condoleezza Rice (*right*) is sworn in as secretary of state in 2005.

Honoring Her Roots

As a member of the K'awaika Nation, Deb Haaland learned to value natural resources such as land and water. She brought these values with her when she served in Congress.

Deb Haaland gives a talk to honor Native American heritage in 2022.

She challenged the use of fossil fuels and their harm to
the environment. In 2021 Haaland became the first Native
American secretary of the interior. She also led the launch
of the Missing and Murdered Unit, which looks into crimes
against Indigenous peoples and works to right the wrongs
committed.

CHAPTER 2

Women in the Legislative Branch

Like Haaland, many women work in Congress to build a better future for everyone. The House of Representatives and the Senate make up the legislative branch. Congress makes laws and plays an important role in the government.

Speaking Up

Nancy Pelosi was the first woman Speaker of the House. Pelosi has been a member of the House for more than thirty-five years. From 2007 to 2011 and 2019 to 2023, Pelosi set the House's legislative agenda, controlled committee assignments, and decided when votes would be held. She also worked to make sure her political party (the Democratic Party) worked together. She fought hard to get the Affordable Care Act passed. It offered affordable health care to millions of US citizens.

Nancy Pelosi speaks at a news conference in 2022.

Fighting Discrimination

Patsy Mink fought for women's rights.

In 1964 Patsy Mink became the first woman of color and the first Asian American woman elected to the House. As a representative, she coauthored the Title IX Act. This act protects people from gender and sexual discrimination in an education program that receives money from the federal government. In 1972 Mink was the first Asian American to run for president. Mink lost the race but talked about the importance of not having wars. She died in 2002, and Title IX was renamed in her honor. In 2014 she was awarded the Presidential Medal of Freedom for her work on Title IX.

Supporting Veterans Rights

Tammy Duckworth served the nation in the military and in Congress. She was a helicopter pilot and became a lieutenant colonel in the National Guard. In 2004 Duckworth earned a Purple Heart for her service. After the military, Duckworth

Tammy Duckworth waves at the crowd during a talk in 2012.

worked to help other soldiers. In 2012 Duckworth became
the first disabled woman and the first Thai American woman
elected to Congress. She continues to help soldiers and
veterans by fighting for them in Congress.

Fighting for Democracy

In 2019 Liz Cheney became the highest-ranking woman in the House Republican leadership. She was an important part of her political party. On January 6, 2021, Congress was attacked by a violent group of people. They thought Donald Trump won the 2020 presidential election.

Cheney became vice chair of the committee looking into the attack. People in her political party weren't happy with Cheney for speaking up. They removed her from leadership. She didn't win reelection in 2022, but she stood up for what she believed in.

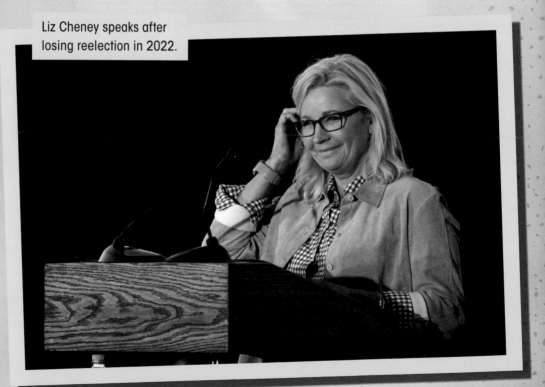

Liz Cheney speaks after losing reelection in 2022.

CHAPTER 3

Women in the Judicial Branch

Women in the judicial branch uphold laws.

On the bench, they also make sure the Constitution is being followed. These women solve conflicts and protect people's rights. They serve in state and federal courts, and the US's highest court, the Supreme Court.

Leading from the Bench

In 1981 Sandra Day O'Connor became the first woman on the Supreme Court. She played a key role in many Supreme Court cases. She voted to support access to education for diverse students and protect the environment against pollution. In 2009 she was awarded the Presidential Medal of Freedom for her leadership and service.

Sandra Day O'Connor served as a Supreme Court justice from 1981 to 2006.

Ruth Bader Ginsburg (*second from left*) is sworn in as a Supreme Court justice in 1993.

Powerful Dissents

Ruth Bader Ginsburg fought for women's rights. She faced gender discrimination while attending law school and practicing law. On the bench, she voted for gender equality in a case where women were not allowed to attend an all-male military institute. She was known for writing powerful dissents, reasons for not agreeing with the majority vote. She wrote a dissent that outlined the history of racial discrimination in voting and why additional protections were needed to create equal access to the ballot box.

Sonia Sotomayor stands next to a bust of herself in 2022.

Considering Cases

Sonia Sotomayor is the third woman and first Hispanic person to serve on the Supreme Court. After graduating at the top of her class, Sotomayor worked at the district attorney's office in New York City and taught at law schools. She joined the Supreme Court in 2009. She is known for speaking her mind. Sotomayor protected people's access to health care

FROM CLERK TO JUSTICE

Amy Coney Barrett was a law clerk for Supreme Court justice Antonin Scalia. She later became a law professor at Notre Dame Law School, where she attended law school. In 2020 she became the fifth woman to serve on the Supreme Court.

At forty-eight years of age, Amy Coney Barrett became the youngest woman Supreme Court justice.

and helped make marriage legal for people of all sexualities. She wrote the dissent in a case about illegal police stops and searches. She said it went against people's rights.

Ketanji Brown Jackson (*front*) signs an oath to become a Supreme Court justice in 2022.

One of the Firsts

In 2022 Ketanji Brown Jackson became the first Black woman appointed to the Supreme Court. She was a public defender and vice chair of the US Sentencing Commission. She was a law clerk for Supreme Court justice Stephen Breyer, who she replaced with her appointment to the bench. Jackson started her first term asking hard questions and writing a strong dissent.

> **"There are also women I have never met but who are recorded in the pages of history and whose lives and struggles inspire me and thousands of other working women to keep putting one foot in front of another every day."**
>
> —KETANJI BROWN JACKSON

CHAPTER 4

Women around the World

All across the world, women are making a difference in government. As of January 1, 2023, thirty-four women were heads of state or government in thirty-one countries. These women are working on such issues as creating access to education, supporting voting rights, and promoting world peace.

Making Her Mark

In 2017 Jacinda Ardern became prime minister of New Zealand. At thirty-seven years old, she became the country's youngest leader. She worked to address many challenges such as immigration, poverty, and reforming gun laws. Ardern started working in politics at the age of seventeen. She later worked in British prime minister Tony Blair's cabinet. She was elected president of the International Union of Socialist Youth and traveled around the world working with other youth leaders.

Jacinda Ardern served as New Zealand's prime minister from 2017 to 2023.

PROMOTING COMMUNITY BUILDING

In 2010 Laura Chinchilla became the first woman president of Costa Rica. She served many leadership roles in government throughout her career. In each role, she worked to improve the lives of everyday people by creating jobs and investing in education. She has also been a leader in environmental justice by working to address pollution in the ocean.

Laura Chinchilla during an interview in 2010

NOBEL PEACE PRIZE HONOREE

In 2006 Ellen Johnson Sirleaf was the first woman democratically elected head of state in Africa. She promoted peace and unity after Liberia's civil war. She was awarded the Nobel Peace Prize in 2011.

Ellen Johnson Sirleaf speaks in front of world leaders in 2017.

Fighting for Health Care

Samia Suluhu Hassan became Tanzania's first woman vice president in 2015. She became president of Tanzania in 2021. She was the fifth African female head of state to address the United Nations. She spoke about the importance of improving access to health-care resources, including vaccinations. She is also working to create jobs and strengthen the nation's economy.

Samia Suluhu Hassan (*center*) receives an award in 2023.

CONCLUSION

Taking Action

Women are making a difference by serving in the government. They fight for justice, equality, and liberty for all. You can also become involved in government. You can go to a city council meeting and write your elected officials about an issue you care about. You can represent students at your school by joining your student government or talking to school leaders. You have your own voice, and you can make it heard.

You can become a leader by speaking up on important issues.

Glossary

congress: the group of people who are responsible for making the laws of a country in some kinds of government

constitution: the system of beliefs and laws by which a country is governed

election: voting that decides who will govern locally or nationally

executive branch: the branch that is in charge of enforcing the law in the US. It includes the president, vice president, executive offices, and the cabinet.

judicial branch: the branch that is in charge of deciding on the meaning of laws and how to apply them in the US. It includes the courts, especially the Supreme Court.

legislative branch: the branch that is in charge of making US laws. It includes the House of Representatives and the Senate.

political party: a group of people who work together to control the government

politics: the act of governing and overseeing a country

prime minister: the head of state in some types of government

Source Notes

4   Merissa Melton, "Shirley Chisholm's Groundbreaking Run for President," VOA, August 14, 2020, https://www.voanews.com /a/2020-usa-votes_shirley-chisholms-groundbreaking-run -president/6194403.html.

7   "Kamala Harris: The Vice President," White House, accessed February 8, 2023, https://www.whitehouse.gov/administration/vice-president -harris/.

22   "NASW Congratulates Judge Ketanji Brown Jackson Her Historic Appointment, Confirmation to the U.S. Supreme Court," National Association of Social Workers, news release, April 7, 2022, https:// www.socialworkers.org/News/News-Releases/ID/2436/NASW -congratulates-Judge-Ketanji-Brown-Jackson-her-historic -appointment-confirmation-to-the-US-Supreme-Court.

Learn More

Banting, Erinn. *Kamala Harris*. New York: Lightbox Learning, 2023.

Boxer, Elisa, and Laura Freeman. *A Seat at the Table: The Nancy Pelosi Story*. New York: Crown Books, 2021.

Britannica Kids: Ruth Bader Ginsburg
https://kids.britannica.com/kids/article/Ruth-Bader-Ginsburg/632200

Britannica Kids: Tammy Duckworth
https://kids.britannica.com/kids/article/Tammy-Duckworth/634076

Doerfler, Jill, and Matthew J. Martinez. *Deb Haaland: First Native American Cabinet Secretary*. Minneapolis: Lerner Publications, 2023.

Ducksters: Sonia Sotomayor
https://www.ducksters.com/biography/women_leaders/sonia _sotomayor.php

National Geographic Kids: Shirley Chisholm
https://kids.nationalgeographic.com/history/article/shirley-chisholm

Schwartz, Heather E. *Ketanji Brown Jackson: First Black Woman on the US Supreme Court*. Minneapolis: Lerner Publications, 2023.

Index

Photo Acknowledgments

Image credits: Universal History Archive/Universal Images Group/Getty Images, p. 5; Sarah Silbiger/Bloomberg/Getty Images, p. 7; Win McNamee/Getty Images, p. 8; AP Photo/Bill Clark/CQ Roll Call, p. 9; LUKE FRAZZA/AFP/Getty Images, p. 10; AP Photo/Susan Walsh, p. 11;; Anna Moneymaker/Getty Images, p. 13; AP Photo/Maureen Keating/CQ Roll Call, p. 14; Joe Raedle/Getty Images, p. 15; AP Photo/Jae C. Hong, p. 16; Charles Ommanney/Getty Images, p. 18; Mark Reinstein/Corbis/Getty Images, p. 19; Matthews Bebeto/Pool/ABACA/Shutterstock, p. 20; Erin Schaff/The New York Times/Bloomberg/Getty Images, p. 21; Fred Schilling/Collection of the Supreme Court of the United States/Getty Images, p. 22; STEVEN SAPHORE/AFP/Getty Images, p. 24; Andrew Harrer/Bloomberg/Getty Images, p. 25; Monica Schipper/Getty Images for Bill & Melinda Gates Foundation/Getty Images, p. 26; PHILL MAGAKOE/AFP/Getty Images, p. 27; Hill Street Studios/Getty Images, p. 29.

Design elements: Old Man Stocker/Shutterstock; MPFphotography/Shutterstock; schab/Shutterstock.

Front cover: Hum Images/Alamy; Tim Graham/Alamy; AP Photo/M. Spencer Green.